COOL COMPETITIONS

Awesome

VIDEO GAME
COMPETITIONS

BY LORI JEAN POLYDOROS

Raintree is an imprint of Capstone Global Library Limited,
a company incorporated in England and Wales having its registered office at
264 Banbury Road, Oxford, OX2 7DY – Registered company number: 6695582

www.raintree.co.uk
myorders@raintree.co.uk

Edited by Aaron Sautter
Designed by Kyle Grenz
Picture research by Eric Gohl
Production by Steve Walker
Printed and bound in China

ISBN 978 1 474 74460 7
22 21 20 19 18 17
10 9 8 7 6 5 4 3 2 1

British Library Cataloguing in Publication Data
A full catalogue record for this book is available from the British Library.

Acknowledgements
We would like to thank the following for permission to reproduce photographs:
AP Photo: Charlie Riedel, 29, Invision for NBA 2K/Dan Steinberg, 25; Getty Images: Bloomberg,
26, Chesnot, 23, Francois Guillot, 14, Sergei Fadeichev, 17, Stringer/Cedric Ribeiro, 20; Newscom:
EPA/Bartlomiej Zborowski, 9, EPA/Paul Zinken, 10, MAXPPP, 13, picture-alliance/dpa/Paul
Zinken, 11; Shutterstock: adamziaja.com, 7, Blan-k, cover (right), MSSA, cover (left & back), Paul
Stringer, 19, Roman Kosolapov, 5

Every effort has been made to contact copyright holders of material reproduced in this book.
Any omissions will be rectified in subsequent printings if notice is given to the publisher.

0517/CA21700461 042017 4655

CONTENTS

READY . . .
SET . . . PLAY!

▶ The lights dim in the arena. Music rumbles and the crowd cheers. On stage, an explosion crashes on the big screen. The game is on! At live video game contests, professional players use quick **reflexes** and smart moves to win.

reflex – action that is performed without conscious thought

FACT

The ESL (Electronic Sports League)
Pro League stars the world's best
players and teams.

5

REAL-TIME BATTLES

Millions of fans flock to video game contests around the world. Fans enjoy watching players compete in **multiplayer online battle arena** (MOBA) games. Many big events also feature real-time strategy (RTS) games.

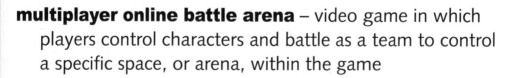

multiplayer online battle arena – video game in which players control characters and battle as a team to control a specific space, or arena, within the game

real-time strategy – video game in which players control a variety of military units and resources to defeat opponents

Huge crowds watch gamers compete at big Intel Extreme Masters events around the world.

Becoming a legend

In *League of Legends*, becoming a legend starts at home. Players first compete on the internet. By winning online, players work their way up the ranks. The top-ranked players can then **qualify** to join professional gaming leagues.

FACT

About 100 million people play *League of Legends* at home every month. It is one of the most popular RTS games in the world.

qualify – to earn a starting place in a competition

Going professional

Top players team up to compete as professionals. The best **squads** can enter the professional gaming series. They compete against other teams in front of live audiences. Screaming fans cheer them on.

squad – group of people who work as a team to achieve a goal

FACT

Winning teams earn money, trophies and other prizes. The *League of Legends* trophy weighs as much as an average eight-year-old child!

FIRST-PERSON COMPETITIONS

▶ Many adult players around the world battle online in the **first-person** shooter (FPS) game *Call of Duty*. These players also compete in global **LAN** events. Winners can earn trophies or cash prizes. They can also win experience points to build up their ranking in the game.

first-person – point of view in video games in which the player sees only what their character sees

LAN – gathering of people who play video games on computers or consoles that have been linked together; LAN stands for Local Area Network

Rising to the top

The highest-ranking *Call of Duty* teams qualify for professional championship **tournaments**. These events are held in Europe, Asia, Australia, and North and South America. The final championship hosts the world's 32 best squads of adult players.

FACT

Winners in the *Call of Duty* championship tournaments earn prizes totalling £1 million.

tournament – series of matches between several players or teams, ending with one winner

Counter-Strike

Adult *Counter-Strike* gamers also move up the rankings by playing online. Teams qualify for the championship through events in Europe, North America and Asia. At the yearly ESL One tournament, teams compete for the title and a £400,000 prize.

FACT

At the 2016 ESL One tournament, fans watched a combined 31 million hours of gaming on the internet.

FIGHTING THE ENEMY

▶ Major League Gaming's (MLG) *Mortal Kombat* tournaments are very popular. In this game, adult gamers fight one-on-one to defeat an opponent's character. To qualify for championships, these players compete online or in live tournaments.

In the *Mortal Kombat X* Pro League, gamers play hard to reach the finals. Players battle through a series of Challenger Cup events. In the final fight, they compete for a £160,000 prize.

Mortal Kombat X Challenger Cup events are held in countries all over the world.

GAME ON!

▶ You don't have to be an athlete to compete at sports games. In *NBA 2K17* players first compete online to move up a **leader board**. With a high enough ranking, gamers can join a professional online team.

leader board – list showing the competitors with the highest scores

Top-scoring *NBA 2K17* teams compete in the "Road to the Finals" tournament. Winning teams keep moving up until they reach the finals. The two highest-ranking teams compete for a big cash prize.

FACT

The *NBA 2K17* championship is held in June at the same time as the real NBA Finals.

Team Drewkerbockers (left) defeated Team GFG (right) to win the *NBA 2K16* championship in 2016.

Madden champions

In the *Madden NFL* American football series, gamers can play in ranked online games to climb the leader board. Top players can then compete in the *Madden NFL* Championship Series.

FACT

The *Madden NFL 17* Championship Series has a total prize pool of £800,000.

BIG-TIME WINNERS

▶ The best gamers have lots of fun while winning huge prizes! South Korea's Sang Hyeok Lee has earned almost £700,000 in *League of Legends* contests. In the United States, former professional gamer Jonathan Wendel won more than $450,000 in prize money.

FACT

In 2016 each member of the Chinese *Dota 2* team took home nearly £1.5 million in prize money.

Jonathan Wendel was entered into the International Video Game Hall of Fame in 2010.

Glossary

first-person point of view in video games in which the player sees only what the character they are playing sees

LAN gathering of people who play video games on computers or consoles that have been linked together; LAN stands for Local Area Network

leader board list showing the competitors with the highest scores

multiplayer online battle arena video game in which players control characters and battle as a team to control a specific space, or arena, within the game

qualify to earn a starting place in a competition

real-time strategy video game in which players control a variety of military units and resources to defeat opponents

reflex action that is performed without any conscious thought

squad group of people who work as a team to achieve a goal

tournament series of matches between several players or teams, ending with one winner

Read more

Coding In Scratch For Games Made Easy,
Carol Vorderman (DK Children, 2016)

Computer Games Designer (The Coolest Jobs on the
Planet), Mark Featherstone (Raintree, 2013)

*Pokémon Deluxe Essential Handbook: The Need-to-Know
Stats and Facts on Over 700 Pokémon,* Cris Silvestri
(Scholastic, 2015)

Website

www.bbc.co.uk/newsround/31767504
Can playing video games help you with your homework?
Find out more about this interesting study.

Index